Each New Sunrise

Each New Sunrise
Meditations in Maturity

by
Margaret Alderman

/ / /

&

SAINT MARY'S PRESS
CHRISTIAN BROTHERS PUBLICATIONS
WINONA, MINNESOTA

With gratitude to Tammy McDowell
who, with patience and encouragement,
taught an old woman to use a computer.

The publishing team included Carl Koch, development
editor; Laurie A. Berg, copy editor; James H. Gurley,
production editor; Cindi Ramm, cover designer; Jill
Rosean Tishman, cover illustration; pre-press, printing,
and binding by the graphics division of Saint Mary's Press.

Printed in the United States of America

Printing: 9 8 7 6 5 4 3 2 1

Year: 2007 06 05 04 03 02 01 00 99

ISBN 0-88489-569-6

Genuine recycled paper with 10% post-consumer waste.
Printed with soy-based ink.

Preface

WE GROW OLDER EVERY DAY AND are aware of the passage of time, of days marking out our later years, and perhaps we experience marked changes in our thoughts. Now stretching toward my fourscore years, I realize that my life outlook has changed, especially in the last four years. In particular my manner of prayer and meditation has altered.

I have been a lover of God since age seventeen when I knew the terror of air raids and the relief of the all-clear. The memory became for me an icon of the relation between pain and joy, death and resurrection. I have been privileged to know godly teachers who willingly shared their love of God and who taught me to work for communication with the Almighty.

In all these years, my spiritual life has been nourished and has grown, but now in maturity, I have found more reflection, more reminiscence, more tranquillity and confidence. During my very active years as wife, mother, widow, and woman religious in two differing confessions, I was more tense about meditation, more concerned about "getting it in." As a member of a religious community, I was privileged to have reserved time for meditation, so the pressure of finding time was absent. Yet the clock was a component of my times with God. There's no telling how much that separated me from my desire to communicate with God. I little appreciated the reflective value of the liturgy and the Divine Office.

I gazed at the sunrise the other morning and suddenly knew that I was out of the "time" routine, out of the pressures, into quiet, peace, serenity, leisurely mulling over small points of the Scriptures and inspirational reading. Lately I have been talking with friends, age peers, who share a small retirement community with me. I have spoken with friends who are blind, bedridden, confined to wheelchairs, in constant pain, and others who are in reasonably good shape. I have talked with them about their faith, about meditation and prayer, and we have shared much. I have heard their courage, their disappointment in living out what some feel are too many days, their yearning for a heavenly rest, for eternity to come. Most of all I have heard hope that things will be better, and I have heard trust in a loving God who graciously hears us and gives us attention, who sends the Spirit to guide and comfort us.

And so the reflections in this book are the fruit of such conversations and of my own experience. To meditate on these reflections, one need only have the book available, pick it up as one can, without pressure, without the need to perform or fulfill an obligation, even without a need to finish the book. My deepest hope is that the reader may share the action of mature souls, those souls that I have discerned in my friends of later years.

Reflections

Differing ideas in the church . . .

are nothing new for believers. Paul found himself faced with serious divisions in the early church, and even asked if he should come to visit with a stick or with gentleness (1 Corinthians 4:21). God has given us a great deal of liberty to find our own best expressions of the Christian faith, with the church as guide and teacher. The important thing to think about is how we respond to the differences we find today, how accepting we can be, how loving, and how our prayers must constantly be made on behalf of any who are troubled in spirit. Give us a generous heart, Divine Teacher, to allow others to exercise the free will that is their birthright.

The old prayer book . . .

is tattered and worn now, and it isn't used much anymore. It is comforting to hold it from time to time, just to feel its softness, to remember how the words have become embedded in one's heart. When one holds an old prayer book, one may remember how it was received and who gave it. Little notes and cards drop out from between the pages, and looking at these mementos, one remembers friends and times of sorrow or joy. What a feeling of peace when returning that old book to its honored place on the shelf. It is good to remember moments that have focused on the love of God. May this build through our remaining days, and let us pray for remembrance of holy times, to be embraced in love.

Am I living in a sinless community . . .

where no one needs forgiveness or the grace of making things right? Are there no compelling inner pangs of conscience to bring the people to repentance at this time? Forgiveness is like a fountain of living water. To explore one's inner self, to ask for forgiveness, and then to receive it—wonder of wonders! Let us never forget that we need this grace of forgiveness to make our way, day by day. Let us never forget that God is being very patient with us, desiring no one to be lost who wants to come to repentance (1 Peter 3:9).

The new translations of the Bible . . .

can be a little confusing. Advice may be needed to discern the most sensible version for a person to use today. The New Jerusalem Bible seem a good choice, worth considering. Personally I have a number of different translations: Knox, the English Bible, Revised Standard, and my old King James. These all sit on the shelf because I can't bear to throw them away. Change is hard, and I resist it. Novelty is no reason for change; Paul warned the Romans not to make changes for novelty alone, but to allow the renewal of mind to transform so that what is good and acceptable may be discerned (Romans 12:2). May we pray for openness to change, for change means we are alive and growing. When the human spirit fights against new ways, may we have strength to find the true good.

Devotions are held every day . . .

here, but so few are present. It is always the same folks, and they do not fill the provided chairs. Many are empty. Yet this is a faithful remnant. Like the monks who all day, every day pray the prayer of the church. Like the faithful communicants of a parish—always present at the Lord's table. Isaiah promises that a remnant will return to the mighty God (Isaiah 10:21). Is it right to admire the remnant and not join them? If one cannot be a physical presence, one may look inward and become spiritually present. For this we pray: to live as part of the faithful remnant, to have courage to support the others, to perpetuate the devotional services, to do more than just a minimum.

Someone has to be in charge . . .

of the church supper that occasionally comes along. We have enough generous hearts to take care of this task, yet sometimes the same person does all the work. I knew a woman, a good woman, who always took charge. She told me at one potluck to cut up my chickens into smaller pieces so that there would be more. I was rather miffed at her bossy tone as I responded that I had brought meat loaf. I failed to consider how hard she worked to make the suppers a success. Now I hope, in these days long after, to appreciate her and to make it up to her in heaven.

During a church service . . .

one may look toward the sanctuary, and
it seems to be covered with angels—so many
that the vessels on the altar can scarcely be
seen. Matthew 16:27 tells of the Savior
coming in glory, with the angels, at the time
of judgment. The angels perceived on the
table are a reminder of God's glory every-
where, at all times, and especially at times
of worship. Angels are quite popular now.
Many friends wear little angel pins, and
perhaps as they wear these, they recognize
that someday they may be with the angels.
Send us your angels, Holy One, to guide us
and guard us and encourage us.

When I went to counseling . . .

for a while, I used to speak of religious matters in connection with feelings that I expressed to the counselor. One time I spoke of how much I wished to follow the will of God in my life. I spoke of how important that was to me. The counselor surprised me by telling me that it wasn't rational to make deals with God. I attempted to explain, but we had no base of understanding. I continued for a few sessions to avoid hurting her, but I soon stopped going. As a matter of fact, God has made a deal with us, a covenant sealed with honor and faithfulness. Genesis 9:16 reminds us of the rainbow, the sign of the covenant. I need to remind myself often that I have made a deal with God, and I must keep it.

Our new membership class . . .

has just been baptized and received. They are a mixed lot, all ages, but all with the same shining faces, happy and peaceful. The parish congregation is enthusiastic in welcome, and there I sit in the pew with tears streaming down my face! I am overcome with gratitude to God, with a heart so full it spills over. I remember my own day, the day I embraced the faith and my life was changed forever. Thank you, God, for these new parish members, for the good teachers who instructed them, and for the sponsors who supported them and prayed for them.

Our new associate pastor . . .

has been with the congregation for a year as an intern, assisting at Communion, doing some of the sermons, working with youth, and endearing himself to all of us, especially the elders. He looks so fine in his robes, and there is a special shining about him. Many of the seminarians are older, having heard their call to ministry after other careers. Younger or older, each year given to us by these servant leaders is a jewel in Christ's crown. I sing in thanksgiving and play the harp for our God (Psalms 147:7). How I pray for these good people who come to us when the church is so in need of them, who hear and answer the call.

These days
I fumble the pages . . .

of the books and hymnals when I am at
worship. I used to have real dexterity with
my hands and fingers, but now I can't seem
to separate the pages when I am looking for
things. I feel that everyone is looking at me,
and I am embarrassed to be so clumsy. So
I say a quick little prayer: "Oh, let me be
patient with myself. Let me not give up, let
me keep trying." So many things that were
commonplace and easy are harder and go
more slowly now. I am acting my age, and
it isn't something to which I have become
adjusted. May we be patient with everyone,
including ourselves, allowing us all to keep
on trying.

Looking through an old Bible, . . .

I was shocked to see how many times I had
written in it, underlined phrases, and made
notes in the margins. I looked at my old
prayer book in which I had done the same. I
don't do that to my newer Bible or spiritual
books. And I wondered what had triggered
those impulses in the past, which perhaps
was not operating in me now. It must have
been that at those times of making notes,
I had felt close to the Holy Spirit, felt a
particular grace granted, and wanted to
preserve the memory, the memory of grace.
Perhaps now, as I have added years upon
years, I have known grace to be more of a
constant in my life, not less memorable but
more obviously present in the day to day.
May the sweetness of receiving gifts of the
Spirit enlighten our daily lives and give us
peace and hope.

Daily obligation to prayer . . .

has been part of my life as a Benedictine oblate in two different confessions, two different churches. It is a good thing to join in the prayer of the church, the church that prays constantly as Paul advised (1 Thessalonians 5:17). Great peace comes in knowing that around the world, day and night, week after week and year after year, the praise and thanksgiving reflected in the psalms goes on without ceasing. To join in the prayer of the church, to find the joy, confidence, and serenity that are promised, is a great opportunity to draw closer to God.

Cracking the Bible . . .

is an act that I have often seen among my friends, and I admire the way those friends rely on the messages perceived. If I were to do that, I would have to have a commentary, a concordance, and perhaps an encyclopedia. It is not that I question the practice of cracking the Bible and trusting whatever passage turns up, but I know myself. I am not satisfied just to read a line or two, but must read at least a chapter or a section to ferret out the context and the story. But in whatever way the Scriptures are interwoven with our lives, it is very good to have the Bible in our hands. How blessed we are that the message and the lessons of the Scriptures may be part of our daily plans and actions.

As a child in Sunday school, . . .

I memorized an uncounted number of Bible verses. Oh, I can still remember them: the verse, the book, and the verse number. The verses are so deep within me that I find them coming to my mind and lips unbidden. It is comforting to remember these tributes to Sunday mornings on a hard bench. That bench was the place where we always moved over slightly so that there was a seat for Jesus. This seems simplistic, but it has meant growth of the feeling that Jesus is beside me. I can count on that Presence always. Let all lovers of God know the constant presence of the Divine. May we recall to mind and heart the important message of the Bible, nothing "in all creation, will be able to separate us from the love of God in Christ Jesus" (Romans 8:39).

Onlookers might wonder . . .

how individual status is gained and maintained in a small retirement community. With apartments in proximity and cottages clustered on the grounds, how do people avoid being one of the crowd? It is surprising to find that position and status in community comes not from activity, nor from outgoingness, but from the attention a resident receives from his or her own family. Residents with no family visits are often lonely, and in that state, they frequently turn to God for comfort. Engrave us on the palms of your hands, Yahweh (Isaiah 49:16), so that our status is as one of your own.

So many loved ones have gone . . .

before into eternity, and as the list lengthens, one looks at percentages: now half of one's beloveds are in heaven, now a little more than half—a strange way of encouraging oneself about the time soon to come when one may join them. Earthly separations give us pain, and over time repetition of the pain of loss may cause us to despair. Yet God has promised and Jesus has won for us eternal life, where separations are no more. Please, my dear God, instill in us through your spirit a strong faith that may carry us into your arms.

My next-to-last first cousin . . .

died today. I remember her as a woman of grace, courtesy, and kindness. I did not live nearby, so I was not able to see her often. She was a part of my childhood and was important to me. I have one more first cousin who lives not far from me and with whom I visit and speak on the phone. She, too, is older, and I know that one day she will be gone. This stripping is part of growing old. We experience it in many ways: moving to smaller spaces and ridding ourselves of excess, losing some agility and talents, knowing new physical limitations. As I experience the stripping, let me raise one hand toward heaven and know that as I lose earthly concerns, I reach more closely above.

❦

Some of my friends . . .

are like part of my family now. As the
family of origin grows smaller, one tends
to replace the empty spots in the heart with
close friends. How fortunate we are to have
friends. In a close community of age peers,
friendships are frequent and strong. We
look out for one another, and when one
says, "How are you?" it is not an empty,
formal phrase. As the Bible says: "Faithful
friends are a sturdy shelter: whoever finds
one has found a treasure. . . . Faithful
friends are life-saving medicine" (Ecclesias-
ticus 6:14–17). There is a family feeling and
an ease with friends—priceless. Let me
always be alert to those who are seeking
friends, and let me embrace them in Christian fellowship and love.

❦

The family Christmas celebration . . .

seemed shallow and empty for the most part. Weather kept some members away, and while the middle-aged relatives and the young were warm and welcoming, something was missing. At the table no grace was said, and throughout the day no mention of the meaning of Christmas was made. It was all Santa Claus and pleasure in gifts, but not a word for the Babe who brought salvation to the world. Give me courage, Best Friend, to defend your place in the Christmas story. When no one else worships you, let me worship you not only in silence. "Glory to God in the highest heaven, and on earth peace!" (Luke 2:14).

❀

The doctor gives me . . .

a serious prognosis, an expectation of future surgery and hazard to health. I sit and ponder the possibilities. I know that this may mean more dependence on close family, yet I procrastinate in telling them. Should I tell them now before this happens? I tend not to want to bear the burden alone, but is it fair for me to shift the anxiety to others? This sort of dilemma has to be prayed out, meditated on, and worked through, trying to see God's direction in all of it. Perhaps I should not ask for a sign; perhaps I had best just pray for light to make a decision that is fair and considerate. Thus I pray.

⚭

Family photos on shelves . . .

get rearranged often. The frames are of all
sizes, and sometimes one gets a new photo
for which room must be made. There are
photos of weddings, graduations, baptismal
gowns, and pets. Some are from many years
ago, even some of myself as a small child.
The photos remind me of continuity, of
generations following after. Neighbors here
have myriad photos—on the walls, on
bookcases, on shelves. These photos help us
to feel less alone, less separated. The
psalmist credits God with generosity in
giving people a home (Psalm 68:10), and so
we follow the example by keeping loved
ones with us. Thank you, God, for setting
the solitary people in families and for the
blessings you have poured upon us. As one
glances at photos, let us breathe a prayer for
each one in them.

My grown children . . .

are very busy people, and I am proud of what they do, occupationally and for others. One lives far away, and I see him rarely. He doesn't phone or write often. I have no reason to believe that he doesn't love me, but he is busy most all the time. I wish I had a bit more priority, but I can't control that. My daughter lives nearby, but works at a difficult job requiring much overtime. Her schedule is such that I must find ways to contact her. So I do that, and she responds whenever she is able. Give me confidence to allow my children their liberty and grace so that I do not feel left behind. Give me strength to do my part to maintain contact.

When my daughter was born, . . .

I named her for and dedicated her to Mary, mother of Jesus. I hoped that she would become imbued with the virtues of Mary, and that Jesus' mother would protect and guide my daughter. I think that has happened, for although there have been trials and difficulties, my daughter has remained kind, forgiving, and gentle. Great devotion to Jesus and his family is present among the elderly. So many have a family history of devotion. Everyone has times when they ask for divine intercession. Holy One, guide and protect all of us who rely on you, and we promise in return to remain devoted.

✤

One of the men in our community . . .

confided to me: "I just pace the floor and wander around the apartment feeling lost. My wife is gone. It was a long illness, and thank God, I was able to be with her and to care for her. But after so many years of being a couple, it is as if half of me is gone. Neighbors stop in, some of the women bring little things to eat, and I am grateful. But I can't bring myself to go over to the common areas, though friends urge me to go to the card games and socials. I will, in time, but some of the pain has to go away. As a rule the man in a couple dies first. I wonder why that is not so in my case." Dear Friend, help me to be grateful for the good years of a happy marriage, to not regret your will in separating us, and to believe that there is more living for me to do—and for my friends, too.

The sliding glass door . . .

helps me to look out on the world, but it also brings in brilliant sunshine. I have to close the drapes against the glare. I used to love the sun and enjoy being out in it, but even with heavily tinted dark glasses, I squint and turn aside. I know that this happens to us as we grow older, but it seems to be one more part of the stripping that pursues us. Peter reminded the Apostles of the prophet's declaration that young men shall have visions, and old men shall have dreams through the Spirit (Acts of the Apostles 2:17). Holy Spirit, preserve me from unclear vision or from turning away from the Light. Give the light of grace to my friends who can no longer see with the eyes of the body.

Pain is a constant companion . . .

these days—will it ever be less? The doctor says that there is no remedy and that the pain will not lessen. I dislike having to take medication, but I must or I would be in misery. When the pills aren't helping, as sometimes happens, I try to remember that I have another constant companion, Jesus, who is always with me. Then I ponder the Resurrection, which gave life to the world, and I try to join myself with Jesus in suffering—and rising. Jesus, friend of these last years, stay by me until I, too, may share in the glory of the Resurrection.

Jar lids are such a problem . . .

for aging hands and wrists. One tries to avoid buying anything that requires the twisting of a lid. Gadgets help, but even those call for certain strength no longer to be counted on. And the plastic bags in which many products are packaged are really tough. With those it takes scissors to get at the contents. Psalm 102 tells of strength failing on the journey, and then offers a prayer that is surely mine, too: "Hear my prayer, O LORD: let my cry come to you. Do not hide your face from me in the day of my distress. Incline your ear to me." Hear my prayer, my God.

❧

Health is a primary concern . . .

for older people. It is a frequent topic of
conversation, and whenever a speaker
comes to touch on a health issue, the atten-
dance and interest are great. I think about
my health too much. I try to tell myself that
I am ready for heaven, but I know that I
am not. The worry perhaps helps me to eat
better and exercise more. Doctors' visits are
frequent and consume much of a senior's
time. Let us focus more on the positive
aspects of our lives, realizing that our physical condition is only one part of life, leaving the whole of our lives in God's loving
hands as we recall God's words, "I am the
LORD, I have called you. . . . I have
taken you by the hand and kept you"
(Isaiah 42:6).

❦

Movers are at a neighbor's apartment . . .

today. That means that he has gone to the next higher level of care, whether it is more living assistance or nursing care or even to the hospital. Independence goes with the cottages, but from time to time circumstances change, and we must rely more on the help of others. My neighbor will be missed, as will his cheery greeting. We hope that he is not suffering or very ill. Often we never see these folks again, and we add them to the number of those who have gone before. God, be good to my neighbor. Help him to grow and be happy wherever you have taken him. Help him to find others so that he will not be lonely or afraid. May he be "straining forward to what lies ahead, . . . toward the goal of the heavenly call of God in Christ Jesus" (Philippians 3:13–14).

Checkpoints, lots of them, . . .

are needed to keep me on track and at my tasks. Care must be taken to put items in the accustomed place and to develop a routine that may be followed. Leaving the house, I return two and three times to make sure I have turned off the stove. I forget to pick up things that I want to take with me, and I have to go back. My short-term recall is faulty. I cannot remember new information. Only time-tested thoughts remain accessible. Divine Teacher, I am grateful for the early years when I learned Bible truths and Christian ways from you; these are so present to me now, with newer memory fading. May you always be present to strengthen us as our faculties dim.

More and more these days, . . .

I look back over my life, over the struggles and the triumphs, and while I can recall events that have brought sorrow or pain or feelings of loss, I see that my life has been blessed by the presence of God. I am so grateful for the gift of faith that has been responsible for this blessing. How sweet to be near the end of my days and to see that they have been good. There is no better proof of your power and love than to see in retrospect. Please allow me to remain with you through the rest of this journey. "My soul magnifies the Lord, and my spirit rejoices in God my Savior . . . for the Mighty One has done great things for me" (Luke 1:46–49).

The Scriptures tell us . . .

of creation groaning in its pains of labor,
waiting to be freed into the glorious freedom
of the children of God (Romans 8:19–22).
Even now we are responsible for doing a
share of the work of bringing creation into
completion. And so we do our best to care
for our earth and its being. The recycling
bins in storage rooms are filled and refilled.
Tender care is lavished on small gardens.
Water and other resources are conserved.
We look about and beg that we may be
given strength and courage to persevere in
the holy work of redeeming this world.

I look around at my possessions: . . .

furniture, books, household goods, clothing, and I wonder what will happen to all this when I am gone. I have made a small rule: anything that I have not used for a year is given away or disposed of. Lately I have been selling and trading books that I have held for thirty-odd years. Suddenly they seem to mean less to me than before. What will others do with this accumulation? Rummage sales are important ways to cut down our baggage. One must, however, beware of bringing home more things! Unlike the rich young man who turned away from Jesus' invitation because he was burdened with too many things, may I be willing to forgo my possessions and turn toward eternity.

The year 2000 is approaching.

I never wanted to live until that late date,
but it appears that I may be destined to see
the turn of the century. Some of my friends
regret the lengthening of their years. As they
approach fourscore and ten years, they feel
weak and long for rest. Yet as their bodily
strength has dissipated, they have gained
wisdom. How very much I have learned
from these people! To be with them is a
school of life. They feel that they have lived
too long, but their days are a revelation
to me. Wisdom from on high, as my days
lengthen and seem long, give me your Spirit
so that your grace is in these last days as it
was in the first. You, my God, "desire truth
in the inward being; therefore teach me
wisdom in my secret heart" (Psalm 51:6).

❧

It was game night, . . .

and we were each engrossed in our favorite pastime when a newcomer arrived. She didn't know how to play the games but wanted to be part of the fun. My partner and I accepted her into our game and told her that we would teach her. Her memory was very bad, and she didn't understand what we were doing. But we stuck with her, and she enjoyed the time. True, we did not have our usual competition, but we had the joy of seeing her happiness at acceptance. We learned this from the Scriptures (Romans 15:1–2). God, give us patience with our friends. In the little ways that we can, may we help another to enjoy life, not pleasing ourselves but supporting one another.

❧

There is a special celebration . . .

for Older Americans Day. Everyone who is ninety years and over gets special recognition. Last year a 103-year-old man was honored. This year he will not be with us at the party, but it is certain he will be in the thoughts of all. He has gone to God in peace and love. As we see these dear ones leave, one by one, we put them in a corner of the heart. We pray that our departed friends are eating and drinking in the Kingdom (Luke 22:30), and that one day we may see them again. Rest in peace.

✄

Several of us volunteered . . .

one day at the local agency that provides food and shelter to street people. We were there through one meal and helped to serve. I watched one man who had finished the beef stew. He scraped the bowl until it was polished and clean. No one knew the stories of those we served. I reflected that many people seem to have the idea that those who are poor are also lazy. The Bible, in Proverbs 6:10–11, declares, "a little folding of the hands to rest, and poverty will come upon you like a robber." Well, we all know that people are poor for a million reasons, many having nothing to do with laziness. As we grow older, we find ourselves experiencing a kind of poverty, too. For some of us it's financial poverty, for others a sharp decline in physical abilities. May we never judge the poor as less than we are, please, God.

My neighbor turned away today . . .

when I greeted him as I was out walking.
I felt shunned. Yet I do not know what
burden he was carrying nor what his
thoughts were. I first personalized what I
saw as a slight, but had I truly been looking
for the Christ within my neighbor, I might
have thought of several different reasons for
the act. Perhaps he did not hear or see me,
perhaps he was in sorrow and could not
speak, or perhaps there was some other
reason. Before I decide I am being attacked
or hurt, let me see Jesus first and find a
Christian explanation for all events. Jesus,
help me remember: "Do not judge, so that
you may not be judged. For with the judgment you make you will be judged"
(Matthew 7:1–2).

There is a sure cure for depression, . . .

or the down days. Nehemiah 8:10–12 tells of those who returned from Babylonian captivity. Because that day is sacred to Yahweh, no one is to be sad, but all are to give to others and be joyful. A good deed is like this: to help someone else, especially if that deed is done in secret, is to sanctify the day, to raise the spirits, and to drive away the blues. The exercise of charity will bring a feeling of well-being. Let this be remembered, and sorrow no more.

❧

I have gone to live among strangers . . .

many times in my life. New experiences
have been my lot, and these events have
frequently put me in new places where I
knew no one. I never worried about this
or anticipated being alone and unhappy. I
knew that I would find brothers and sisters
there because I learned from 1 John 4:21
that we are commanded to love our brother
and sister if we love God. So wherever I
may be, I have kin of the Spirit, and I can
be satisfied and fulfilled in coming to know
and love them. May I remember when I say
I love you, God, that my love must reach
out to all.

Walking past apartments . . .

we sometimes see a neighbor, sitting in front of the television, looking alone and depressed. We wish to go to these neighbors and give them a friendly word, but we don't want to reveal that their situation has been seen. Sometimes we can give them a phone call and talk about trivial things. There are too many of these scenes, and it is disturbing. A few people sit in the lobby of the main building here at the residence, day after day, hour after hour. Just to see others. Many speak with them or smile. It seems we are all looking for friends; perhaps that is why the curtains are not closed. Open our hearts, Holy Friend, so the open curtains draw us in to be a friend to the lonely.

Friends ask me to pray . . .

for them or for some special need, or often
they ask me to pray for certain others who
are undergoing trials. Usually the request
is for some specific solution by God to the
troubles and trials that beset us. The number
of requests I get is probably reduced because
I tell the askers that I will pray for God's
will in the situation. It is such a prominent
injunction in the prayer that Jesus taught
(Matthew 6:10). God does for us what is
known to be our need, not necessarily our
desire. May I pray this way and accept the
answer, even if there does not seem to be one.

❧

Violence is abroad in the land . . .

it seems, with terrible stories heard on a daily basis. It is frightening to realize the intensity and frequency of violent acts among ordinary people, attacks on human dignity and freedom. We hear much talk about how to stop the violence, how to put an end to its acceleration. But a basic problem exists: too many people have forgotten or never knew of the great value of the human person (Isaiah 45:12). Somehow we must restore respect for human life. In my smallest action, Giver of Life, let me remember the uniqueness and holiness of my neighbors. Let me honor your Spirit, who dwells in them.

Another neighbor moved away . . .

yesterday. I had not discussed this with her, so I do not know where she went or why she has made a change. It reminds me of the many times that I have changed locations in my life, and I think of pilgrims who move on, searching for something. A traveler is moving, but a pilgrim has a goal (Hebrews 11:16). I pray to continue a pilgrimage toward that heavenly goal, for when we reach that goal, we are travelers and pilgrims no more.

I distrust my first reactions . . .

to things, events, and people. I am no longer as sure of myself as I was when I was younger. I have lived long enough to see the number of times I have blundered by going with my first impulse. Proverbs advises: "Do you see someone who is hasty in speech? There is more hope for a fool than for anyone like that" (29:20). The Apostle James has much more to say about the dangers of snap judgments and quick words. Have I truly learned to step back and to consider and reconsider that one who trusts only in God, not in self, is secure? I hope that this becomes a more constant response. May it be so.

How easy to get lost in memories . . .

these days. As onc ages, faraway and by-gone events seem easier to recall than what happened last week. To stay too much in the past tells me that I do not trust that I have a future, that I don't even look forward to the new sunrise. The remedy for this kind of thinking is found in Galatians 2:20: "It is Christ who lives in me. And the life I now live in the flesh I live by faith in the Son of God." My life lived now must be lived by faith in God. I must concentrate on the "now" of my days, the now of each moment. Let me treasure each new day, each new hour.

After all these years . . .

I am beginning to know myself better
(Colossians 3:9–10). I am finding out that
humility comes hard, even though I have
repeated reasons to learn it. But what is
humility other than knowing oneself to be
mortal clay, dignified and saved only by the
mercy and love of the Creator. For a long
time, I was bound up in concealing my
errors and embarrassments. Now I just lay
them out for my friends and neighbors to
see. It is less difficult to be laughed at now,
and I can even more easily accept the
sympathy of other people. I pray to continue in your school of life, all-good God.

My parents may have . . .

made too much of me when I was a child. They had waited a long time for my birth, and they thought that I was a prize. I remember being a testy kid who became upset when things didn't go my way. Dealing with the world was another matter: I soon learned that if I wished things to go my way, I had to be "smart." So I worked at being smart, and was able to get my way in numerous situations through cleverness and hard work. A couple of things have happened though. I no longer have the energy or the desire to be "smart." I also have come to admire the advice in Philippians 2:3–5: "Do nothing from selfish ambition or conceit, but in humility . . . look not to your interests, but to the interests of others. Let the same mind be in you that was in Christ Jesus." I pray that I will grow into this more and more.

❦

Many of my neighbors . . .

have withdrawn into a shell and will not
participate with others in our community
life. I understand that it is a great change
to come to a community from one's own
home, but as loved ones go on to another
sphere and friends become preoccupied with
their lives, my neighbors need new friends.
I have vowed to relate to the lonely and the
withdrawn insofar as I am allowed to by
them. Please, Heavenly Friend, let me not
cease from trying to be a friend to them, nor
allow me to withdraw from our community
life.

Volunteering has been a big part of my life . . .

since I retired. However, I think that I have gone overboard in making these "just a few hours a month" commitments. Now I am swamped with obligations and responsibilities, so much so that I have to get my life in order. Now I must write down these obligations and balance them with good sense and a realization that I may overextend myself. As the Scriptures tell us in Proverbs 16:3, when God is included, one's plans are realized. Again in verse 9, the human heart may plan, but Yahweh secures the course. May I have recourse to prayer and contemplation as I study a way to manage my ambitions.

Whenever I feel a lack . . .

of something for myself I can look around
and find someone who has what I do not.
Often this comes to mind as I hear people
talking about their stocks, their investments,
the thousands and thousands of dollars they
made by selling their property, and so on. I
have little, and often must stretch my means.
Concentrating on what I lack can lead to
envy. Give me strength to follow the injunc-
tions of 1 Corinthians 13:4, to set aside jeal-
ousy and substitute a feeling of gladness
that someone else is rich.

How easy it is to feel powerless . . .

when one is well aware of declining personal power. Situations arise, and one can only stand back and lament the inability to make any effective difference. Surely homeless people must feel deeply this inability to climb out of difficulties and assume a better position. In 1 Corinthians 4:10, Paul describes his feeling of powerlessness as a fool for Christ: "We are weak, but you are strong. You are held in honor, but we in disrepute." Am I willing to be such a fool? Jesus, help me to accept my limitations but to do what I can for your glory and for the good of my sisters and brothers.

A silver thaw is a deadly thing, . . .

for when the ice sheathes the tree branches and they glisten like crystal, so also are the streets and walks and cars covered with an icy veneer. Branches break, leaving piles of debris when the ice has gone. Where there have been clusters of trees, now there are tangled toothpicks waiting to be cut up and thrown into a fire. Yet the ice melts, the water runs off, spring comes, and the trees burst with buds and new life. In the midst of the silver thaw, help us, Creator, to remember the resurrection of humanity and the hopes for creation. May we never fail to see new life in the midst of death.

Soggy, decomposing, the autumn leaves . . .

lie under the snow. When they fell, God watched them—every one. So it is that God guards and guides us every day of our lives. If we feel alone or downcast, we must make ourselves remember God's tender love for each of us, the sensitivity to every human situation, the rescue from the ignominy of the commonplace. We are special, unique, loved. Let us not forget, as the snows of winter bear us to the ground, that our watchful God is with us: "Now that you have been freed from sin and enslaved to God, the advantage you get is sanctification. The end is eternal life. . . . The free gift of God is eternal life in Christ Jesus" (Romans 6:22–23).

Dear little hungry birds . . .

congregate outside the patio window, hop-
ping about looking for food in the cold day.
I see three different kinds of birds, all little
ones with white breasts and tiny black top-
knots, some with a tinge of scarlet on the
breast. They scatter when I open the door
to throw seeds for them, but soon return to
feast. Others here feed the birds, but I think
the birds who come to my patio depend on
me, as I depend on my heavenly Friend for
spiritual life. Those who rely on Yahweh
will triumph, for there is always godly
support for those who are loyal: "You are
indeed my rock and my fortress. . . .
Into your hand I commit my spirit; you have
redeemed me, O LORD, faithful God"
(Psalm 31:3–5).

The tulip tree is getting ready . . .

to explode in spring glory. The tiny buds are so soft, soft as kitten's fur. One wants to touch and stroke them, thinking about the leaves that will come in little batches and then the blossoms, exotic and exciting. This spring resurgence of life is forever a reminder of death and resurrection. The people complained about Jesus working healing miracles on the Sabbath (John 5:16). In truth, we see the miracles again and again in the tulip tree. It works its healing miracles every day, too. God, in this spring glory, may I be encouraged in healing hope, and be reminded of your constant loving presence, leading us to resurrection.

❧

One of the favorite things to do . . .

here at the residence is to go for rides in the country on the community bus with a good driver. One has plenty of time to look and to enjoy because the stress of driving is absent. This is beautiful country, mostly green and lush with flowers in the spring, summer, and fall. There are many farms around, and the old barns and the animals are joyful to see. Do I look around at my surroundings enough to really see my neighbors, to look into their faces and see heartaches or happiness? God, let me be more aware, and let me take a ride in people country.

I lift up my eyes to the mountains— . . .

where is my help to come from (Psalm 121:1)? How often I raise my eyes to the east of my dwelling and see majestic Mount Hood, one of the Northwest's wonders. It is such a symmetrical mountain, always glistening with snow, and at sunset changing colors every moment. The psalmist tells us that our help comes from Yahweh, who made heaven and earth. It seems easy to realize this help under the shadow of a great mountain. Grace, God's help, is offered at every moment. Help make my heart ready to accept this blessing, this amazing bounty of God.

❦

Each new sunrise . . .

tells us of a new day, another in the string of life that God has provided. As one ages, one has less surety of the new day, and we remember as we fall asleep each night: "Now I lay me down to sleep, I pray the Lord my soul to keep. If I should die before I wake . . ." and it is all very real. When we wake to the sunrise, we are gifted with an untouched day, a day in which all our being is renewed and we may make a mark in the journey to eternal life. This day is a "new creation" (2 Corinthians 5:17). I pray that I greet the dawn with gratitude and with the determination to make the day memorable for someone in need.

I asked a pastor how to pray . . .

without ceasing. He told me about the
Jesus prayer and gave me a pamphlet that
explained it. I followed the directions care-
fully because I had read 1 Thessalonians
5:17, and I truly wanted to pray constantly.
I counted each repetition of this ancient
prayer, "Lord Jesus Christ, have mercy on
me," one thousand times a day, two thousand times a day. After a long time, I stopped
the counting, and the prayer began to live
in me. Now, forty years later, I only notice
when the prayer stops briefly. Thank you,
my teacher from God, for teaching me a joy
that has informed my lifetime.

I know it is time to pray, . . .

but I am drawing a blank. What shall I pray about? I seem to have done enough praying about my concerns. It is time I looked elsewhere for needs. Who is ill? Who is hurting? Who does not recognize a personal relationship with the Almighty? Suddenly I have a huge list of persons and needs, and I have more to pray about than I could have imagined. Cloistered religious face this situation every day, and find enough material to pray about to keep them busy for hours and hours. So they are "alert at all times, praying" (Luke 21:36), and thus they develop a habit of prayer. Keep me faithful to the habit of prayer in Your Name.

This new Catechism is a big book . . .

big not only in the sense of size but also
in its impact on me. I find that I can easily
look up anything I want to know, but it is
especially helpful to me when I am attending
a lecture on, for instance, church history.
The instructors so often refer to the *Cate-
chism* now, and I can read and reread the
points made. I have tried not to read it
chapter after chapter—it overwhelms me.
Some of my friends complain of changes,
but I find few—other than those that move
us as Christians back to the time of the
Apostles for our ground of theology. I like
that. I feel more in tune with those first
preachers and with Christ teaching (Luke
21:37).

Television offers us . . .

a variety of worship programs, many with beautiful surroundings or landscapes. The particular beauty of the setting makes viewing worthwhile. We are often solicited to buy a videotape that would be a permanent memorial of the scene. What a blessing for shut-ins. I thought: "I can just sit here and think about church and worship, easier than dressing and going to church. I should buy the videotape." It struck me that that was too comfortable a way to handle devotions. I must put my heart and my body into it (Colossians 3:23), and I will not buy that tape. I pray to be a more energetic disciple, to put myself out in respect for Jesus' sacrifice.

Outside of praying in church, . . .

it seems to me that walking is the most spiritual act. We read so much about Jesus walking with the disciples, and when we walk in a contemplative mode, we are with them. The things we can learn on a simple walk: things and people and places we might never see, or might never realize that we see. The slowed-down walking mode that age forces us into gives us time to reflect. We cannot always be sure of what we see: look at the disciples on the road to Emmaus (Luke 24:16–17). If we are attentive, we may see Christ revealed to our dimmed sight. I pray that God will give me sufficient strength to walk for many years.

When I check myself on simplicity, . . .

I visualize myself standing before the throne of God, awaiting judgment. A pastor once told me that I tended to get too visual in my meditations and mental meanderings. So I try very hard not to concentrate on the splendor and glory of the throne, but to look into my heart. When I was a novice in the religious community, I asked what simplicity was, for it was a virtue recommended. I was told to be myself. That must mean no pretense, no hedging, no dodging, no blaming someone else. We hear this best in Proverbs 8:8–9: "All the words of my mouth are righteous; there is nothing twisted or crooked in them. They are all straight to one who understands and right to those who find knowledge." Dear God, let me face you just as I am and trust in your mercy and love.

❧

The housekeeper comes to my place . . .

once a week and generally keeps me in order by straightening up and scouring and cleaning. She takes care of the physical space I inhabit, but I am the one who must look after my interior space, my spiritual self. And so I go to confession to be reconciled to God, to promise to pull away from all the matters that separate me from the love of God, to renounce all disorder and once again face toward heaven. May I remember to hold out my hands to the forgiving arms of the church, the community of God's people.

⚘

How well I recall the days of training . . .

as a religious: how hard we struggled against obedience, more often with humor than in any other way, but nevertheless resisting a life filled with orders and suggestions from someone else. Jesus admonished Paul about "kicking against the goads" (Acts of the Apostles 26:14), and surely that is what we did as postulants, and more quietly as novices. After a while it begins to take too much time to protest so much, and the spirit settles down to business. Life now is filled with obedience to unvoiced demands that arise merely from the circumstances of growing old. Let us not kick against the burdens of compliance; let us just rest it all in God and get on with living.

The characters of the Bible . . .

strike me as vital parts of a magnificent panorama of history and teaching. We are invited to almost place ourselves with them. Or, in our mind, we can become one with them. To explore their good qualities and their failings, to consider how we measure up to their lives can be a fine preparation at the beginning of a year or of any enterprise that is directed toward God. Peter is a favorite: he has a great heart filled with good intentions, but he reaches greatness only by grace—and he knows it. Or, Ruth, the model of friendship. Great Teacher, allow us to travel in Bible country and to meet the people there as we would meet old friends.

The old sisters . . .

were always a source of inspiration to me.
I spent as much time with them as possible,
and learned what a life of love can mean.
On Sundays we would check out a car, me
driving, and we would visit a different
shrine or contemplative community chapel
each time. This was what these women
wanted to do on a day off. These sisters had
active lives: all worked a full week—and
more—and although one might think they
would want a break from prayer and spiritual efforts, their preference clearly showed
the depth of their love for Christ. Now that
I am old, too, I feel life's focus changing.
Jesus, let me come close to you in whatever
way I can, as often as I can.

My thoughts are like birds on a wire, . . .

settling, rising, settling again, trying to hold tight to where and who I am. The inability to concentrate for long periods of time interferes with integration, and the fact that I pay too little attention to what I want to remember means that I forget. I must return over and over until the recall comes. I have learned that my optimum orientation to meditation is the word of God, cutting through the confusion of age, and marshaling my thoughts (Hebrews 4:12). Settle me down, Holy One, allow me to focus, clasp me tightly.

Faith came to me as a gift . . .

when I was seventeen and the night was black and frightening, and there was an air-raid alarm. I cowered under the covers of my bed, and when, in a few minutes, the all-clear sounded, I knew that fear and pain would be followed by joy. I knew that God was responsible for that gift through the sacrifice of Jesus. A pastor once told me that if I never doubted, how would I know I had faith? That has proven true, for I have had moments of doubt, but each time that doubt is overcome, I grow more deeply the knowledge of what faith can mean. Moses likened Yahweh to an eagle brooding over the nest (Deuteronomy 32:11). May I always know the surety of that faith secured to me by Christ.

There are many fallen pinecones . . .

on the walk and on the grass. They look so dead, but a secret of life is locked inside. The seeds are hidden life. I try to live the spirituality and devotion of a hermit, even though I live in a busy community. By the door of my home, I have placed the hermit's entrance and exit prayers, and as do devout Jews with their doorposts, I touch the prayers at entrance and exit. Having a secret life of religion is stabilizing and comforting. I read the words of Jesus at the well (John 4:13–14). A hidden prayer life is like the living water offered by God. Thus may I return again and again to the well of solitude and contemplation.

❦

An old woman has time on her hands, . . .

especially if she is confined by disability or illness, and memories become important. Visions of the past crowd her mind, and sometimes she has visions of the future. This seems to follow the prophecy of Joel 3:1–5, speaking of the new age and the day of Yahweh. The Spirit will be poured out, and all who call on the name of Yahweh will be saved. It is as one of the remnant, the poor of Yahweh, that an old woman exists and looks toward the heavenly reward and eternal life. Look down on me, great God of my life, and forgive my sins and lapses, bind me closer to you.

The new sunrise is not so apparent . . .

this morning. It is a cloudy day, and everything is obscured by clouds and fog. Yet I believe that the sun is up there, hidden, still warming us. The hope is born that we will soon see sunshine, for it cheers us. A child was only two years old when his father died, and one day when he was older, he asked his mother how he could love God whom he had never seen. She said, "Do you love your father whom you don't remember seeing?" The boy answered, "Oh, yes." The mother said: "It is the same. You have faith that you had a human father who loved you; now you can love the heavenly Father in the same way." The Light is sometimes behind clouds, but our faith assures us it is there. Even in maturity we are children of the Light.